MW01251561

No Limit Publishing Group
123 E Baseline Road, D-108
Tempe, AZ 85283
info@nolimitpublishinggroup.com

This book was printed in Canada

rhonda@knowyourdifference.com
www.knowyourdifference.com
Design by Aster* Communication Design

know your difference™

rhonda page

When you know your difference, you own your market!

How are *you* different?

Acknowledgments

This book is dedicated to my family...
To my parents Albert and Sandra Page, thank you for your belief in me and being my number one fans. To my sons Matt and Daniel Hoffman, my brother Steven, sister-in-law, Shawna, my nephew Spencer and my nieces Sydney and Skylar Page, thank you for your unconditional love, friendship and support.

With gratitude...
Thank you to all the people who helped me in different ways to birth know your difference™. Each of you brought unique perspectives and contributed to the amazing journey that led me to launch this project.

RICHARD HOFFMAN: thank you for the summer of '86 in Los Angeles that launched my career and thank you for Matt and Daniel. **MICHAEL KOREN:** you took me on an unforgettable adventure that led me to Dossier. You pushed me to become a better version of myself. **SHERREE FELSTEAD, LOIS TUPPER AND JENNIFER KELLY:** thank you for your love, support, ideas and belief in me! Sherree, thank you for your incredible contribution to writing and editing this workbook. **MICHAEL RAHMAN:** for your endless patience, guidance and leading me to the Hoffman Institute, **HELEN VALLEAU:** For your wonderful friendship and inspiration. Thank

you for facilitating the creation of this vision and giving me the tools to realize it. **TOM KUHN:** for our endless business discussions, your faith in me, for your number-crunching and your wonderful friendship. **JENNIFER YOUNG:** for your cheerleading, ideas and input into know your difference™! **JACQUELINE MORIN:** you've kept me laughing...and laughing...and laughing. Bisous. **ROBERT PAL:** for your invaluable marketing and business advice. **BARBARA SCHREINER-TRUDEL:** for your inspirational talks that have kept me moving forward toward my vision. **DON CLELAND:** for your creativity and contribution to the "inside design" portion of the workbook. **DON AND RONNA CHISHOLM AND DOSSIER:** for your mentoring, guidance, inspiration, directing me to Birkman and showing me my clarity. **DAVE PHILLIPS:** thank you for Birkman, sharing your resources and all your wonderful support and coaching. **MEGAN HUNT:** thank you for bringing know your difference™ to life through your wonderful design work. **RACHAEL BELL:** thank you for your great copy editing and contribution to know your difference™. Also thank you to all my wonderful clients over the years who have taught me so much and have become valued friends. **THE HOFFMAN INSTITUTE:** thank you for your great work, I continue to be guided by the light. Last but not least, thank you **NO LIMIT PUBLISHING GROUP:** for showing me there are "no limits."

Author's *note*

This workbook is 20 years in the making. It began with my studies in graphic design at Ontario College of Art & Design in Toronto, Canada and Parsons School of Design in New York City. Upon graduating, I worked for some of the top graphic designers in the world. They taught me the importance of having a clear message aligned with good design.

Clients on the other hand, shared their business problems, and in the end, just wanted a "nice-looking brochure." (This was back in the days when brochures were the most popular form of marketing and advertising.) The concept of having a clear message nagged at me. I used to ask myself, "What was a nice-looking brochure going to do for their business without a message that differentiated them?"

I remember working with a law firm in 2000 that wanted a new corporate image. I asked them to collect the brochures of their competition. When we laid them out on the table, they all looked the same. The words used were slightly different, but nothing stood out that differentiated any of

them. This motivated my client to create a unique identity and marketing materials that really stood out from other law firms. Later, I worked with a construction company that needed a new name. They were being mistaken for a charity. We came up with a list of fabulous names, but in the end, they chose to copy a competitor's name because it was obviously working for them! In the law firm example, they understood what differentiation meant but in the construction company example, they didn't. Copying the competition just creates more noise.

As time went on, clients continuously asked for *pretty design* while design firms struggled to sell them on the merits of "brand strategy": develop a good positioning statement that declares who they are, who they provide products or services for and how they are different; in essence, their Unique Selling Proposition (USP).

I have observed that every brand I've worked on throughout the years—both large and small—struggles with the challenge of differentiating themselves and it's not an easy challenge to overcome.

I've worked on every kind of brand you can think of, from cosmetics and pharmaceuticals, to food, wine, resort real estate and insurance. As I evolved from designer to brand strategist, I asked a lot of questions and tried in my own way to solve clients' problems. Clients often remarked on my ability to give clarity and solve problems creatively. One said that I cut through the crap quickly. According to **THE BIRKMAN METHOD** personality assessment, my problem solving skills are *off the charts!* Training in productive thinking and creative problem solving further refined these skills.

After 13 years of marriage, my husband and I divorced in 2001. Now a single woman with a career and two boys to raise, I began a quest to find peace in my life. I started reading books and taking courses in personal development and studied the works of Louise Hay, Wayne Dyer, Deepak Chopra and many other inspirational leaders. This quest culminated with **THE HOFFMAN PROCESS** in 2009.

My personal work has given me a great deal of insight into people and how they tick. As I continued collaborating with brand teams at various companies, it occurred to me that brand leaders who were the most successful were the ones with a strong vision and a passion for what they do. I also began to see what stands in the way of most people's success: their emotional baggage.

I realized that when people create a brand from a place of authenticity—that is, their inherent values, highest vision and passion—they are not only successful, but fulfilled. They ultimately bring more joy and happiness to the world.

Here are my three wishes for you as you work through this book.

1. *That you achieve great clarity.*
2. *That you create a brand that comes from your passion and vision.*
3. *That you reach the pinnacle of success you have always wanted.*

Love and light, Rhonda

Introduction

How know your *difference*™ got started

It all started in 2008, when the economy declined dramatically and a number of my friends lost their jobs. Many people were out of work and wondered how to get noticed by potential employers or stand out above their competitors to retain or win new business. I was often approached with, "If you can help the big brands differentiate, then you can do it for me." So I developed a process to help my friends know their difference and it worked!

know your *difference*™ became a way for entrepreneurs and small businesses to define their brand as a foundation for growth. It is the culmination of my learning from 20 years in the branding business, where I observed the biggest companies experiencing the same challenge: knowing their difference. Finding a way to stand out in a cluttered marketplace is something we all face. It's like walking through a supermarket aisle and realizing that none of the brands stand out. Which one would you choose?

Whether you're starting a new venture or have experienced success and want to move your business to the next level, this workbook will take you through the steps to gain insight and clarity in defining what makes you different from others who are doing the same kind of work as you.

Most importantly, you will be able to express your difference with confidence and in a way that is engaging to your audience. Your difference will make you stand out and shine!

When you know your difference, you own your market.

www.knowyourdifference.com/breakthrough

My *own* difference

Here's how I talk about know your difference™

know your difference™ is a branding program for the passionate entrepreneur or small business owner who is open to new ways of thinking about their business. The program helps them develop a clear picture of their unique difference and align it with their vision and passion so they can market their business effectively.

What makes me different?
- Big agency "know-how" made available to small businesses.
- The only program of its kind that combines branding principles with personal development techniques.
- A unique business model for the branding industry.

What makes me credible?
- Twenty years experience, working on every kind of brand possible: cosmetics, pharmaceuticals, food and beverage, real estate, financial services, transportation and logistics for global companies like *Kraft* and *Nestlé*.

- A unique background that combines graphic design, brand strategy, business development and personal development.
- A talent for easily clarifying what may seem complex to others.

How will you feel after completing know your difference™?

Clear

How's that? Once you have completed this workbook, you will be able to speak as clearly about your product or service as I have spoken about mine.

Have fun with it!
Rhonda

Table *of* contents

SIX STEPS TO BRAND CLARITY

Story: **Branding is not a logo**

HELEN VALLEAU
VISIONING COACH AND AUTHOR OF
*A year of possibilities: 365 Simple Steps
to Make Your Life a Masterpiece*

My journey into the world of branding began when Rhonda and I were at a silent auction and she saw me bidding on a marketing package. She asked me what I need it for and I told her I was working on a book that helps people create a life of purpose and passion through visioning. I wanted to know how to go about marketing it. She said, "I can help you with that."

Shortly after the silent auction, we actually got together and I showed her the workbook. It was the first time I had ever shown anybody my project and shared my vision for it. Rhonda loved the idea and began working with it.

I had no previous understanding of what branding is. I didn't know what to expect and I had no idea what the outcome was going to be, because it was new territory for me. To be truthful, I thought a logo was branding. But she opened my eyes. She made me aware that everything I do is a reflection of my brand. My brand needs to be authentic and resonate with who I am and how it impacts my target market.

I worked with Rhonda on a consistent basis: going through her branding workbook, doing the exercises, taking her workshop and working with her one-on-one to get very clear about who my target audience is and how the book would benefit them. I remember during her workshop I had a couple of "aha" moments. At first, I thought my book was for those on a spiritual journey. Instead, it turned out to be for people who are 40-plus and in transition for the second phase of their life. The tagline also sprung to life: "create a life of purpose and passion."

It was exciting to know that my vision was becoming a reality. One day Rhonda and I had a half-day work session where we brainstormed different names for the workbook. She came up with the name *"A year of thinking differently."* Once we were set on the name, she told me about a graphic designer who would be perfect to design my book. She said, "I found the perfect designer for you. Call her!" She was really excited. I did and she was right. Working with this designer brought about a number of unexpected opportunities

for me. When we did a trademark search for the name, we discovered that the title of the workbook was already registered by Steve Jobs of Apple Inc! We went back to work and came up with an even better name, *"A year of possibilities."*

All the pieces came together working with Rhonda. What we've done feels very purposeful and meaningful to me. I am very passionate about visioning and I'm doing it, because ultimately, I believe in the power of it. I'm able to bring the process to a sharply focused, grounded, tangible place for people to grab onto.

I believe that what I've developed is really authentic. There were moments when I got off track and I would bring myself back to, "What is my mission here?" Focusing on that and letting the rest fall into place—trusting that the rest will be as it is meant to be and not giving up or compromising what my mission or my passion in life is.

www.ayearofpossibilities.com

What brought you *here?*

"I'm overwhelmed with working hard, but not attracting as many new clients as I would like."
"I'm not clear on where I want to go with my business."
"I have a unique business model, but I'm not sure how to communicate it clearly."
"I have a great offer, but find it hard to communicate how it's different from the competition."
"I have spent thousands of dollars on a website that isn't quite working for me."
"I have 10 years experience and can offer so much, but don't know which service to promote."
"I keep hearing that I need branding help, but I'm not really clear about what the term means."
"I need to figure out my brand so I can get on with my marketing."

I hear the above statements all the time. The simple truth is, if you have competition, you need to put some thought into your brand.

Each person on this earth is unique. We all have a different story and it doesn't matter if you are one of many real estate agents or interior designers. Your skills and talents are unique to you. You may have a kind of intuitive understanding of what makes you different and you are passionate about what you do; however, you cannot assume that others will naturally feel the same way. Often they don't.

This program helps you channel your passion and intuition for what works, and turn your insights and knowledge into practical tools that articulate your difference. It's about making sure other people *get it* the way you do. That's the first step to being successful. Next is living a joyful life in which you put your passion into practice by doing what you love.

You may become aware of fears and anxiety when you start to look deeply into your business, but don't worry. Just acknowledge them and move on. It is part of the process to feel this way. You are embarking on a new journey.

What is a *strong* brand?

A brand is the thought or image that comes to mind when you think of a particular product or service. It is a promise made by a business to its customers. Take for example, Apple Inc. What comes to mind when you think of Apple? When I think of Apple, I think of great design, great service and cool products. What would you like to come to mind when people think of your product or service?

Branding is not a logo, a website, a business card or an ad. However, these are some of the tools you use to express your brand. That's it! Plain and simple.

This workbook takes you through the six steps to brand clarity, guiding you in creating a strong brand by developing a clear and compelling message, and then showing you how to bring your brand to life by creating marketing tools—logo, business cards or website—that are aligned with your message.

Most people are running around trying to get stuff done, "I need a website, I need a logo, etc." Before you do any of those things, you need to know your difference™. Once you know your difference, you have the basis to move forward. Marketing is about getting the word out, but branding is about knowing what the "word" is.

What is a *strong* brand?

A brand that communicates a clear message

A brand that stands out from the competition

A brand that inspires action (and lots of it)

www.knowyourdifference.com/breakthrough

Story: **New name. New identity.**

DIANNE LEBRETTON
CHAIR AND CEO, **ClearShift**
*Working with CEO's to find the way forward
through complex circumstances.*
www.clearshift.ca

Although I am experienced in the area of brand-ing, I was unable to do it for myself. For a number of years I had been on the lookout for someone to help me take my business to the next level – someone "who knew their stuff." When Rhonda presented to my Mastermind group, I could tell she would be able to satisfy my high standards.

One of the first things Rhonda asked me when we began working together was how people reacted to my company name, IpicUs. She had a gut feeling that the name may not be serving me well. We agreed that the only way to know for sure was to ask! She conducted a series of telephone inter-views with nine of my key stakeholders – all CEO's and Executive Directors of large organizations. The interviews revealed insights about my business

that had never crossed my mind. I learned that the promise I thought was relevant to my clients was neither clear nor what they were looking for. It was also confirmed that I needed a new name. In addi-tion to looking at some of the hard facts, I learned about new opportunities for growth.

Rhonda and I then worked together to get clarity on a promise that would link to a new name and logo. When I learned that I would need a new company name, I was quite anxious. I had been operating my business under the current name for 13 years and had invested substantial dollars in trademark, promotion and good will. When your clients tell you that you need a new name, you can't ignore that. I put Rhonda to work to come up with a new name. We were very clear on the positioning of

the business and the name was to flow out of that – and it did! When she presented three names to me, I knew that "ClearShift" was the one. It cap-tured the promise brilliantly. I ran it by a few clients and they said, "That's exactly what you do for me."

The words that I use to describe my business now are fast forwarding the sales process for me. People get it quickly. Rhonda is now leading the creation of my new logo and website. It's exciting to have someone with "big agency" experience working on my brand. The best thing about working with Rhonda is her ability to slice through a lot of mush to find the golden nugget!

Six steps to *brand clarity*

**THERE ARE SIX STEPS TO CREATING
A STRONG BRAND:**

1. *Getting clear on your vision*
2. *Getting clear on your ideal client or customer*
3. *Getting clear on your competition*
4. *Getting insights from your client or customer*
5. *Developing a differentiated message*
6. *Bringing your brand to life*

The process on the following pages should take approximately six to eight weeks to complete. Allow one week to complete each step, with the exception of Step 4. This step requires at least two weeks.

You will need to set aside quiet time to think, reflect and do some informal research. Please follow the instructions carefully and don't skip any of the steps! It will all come together in the end.

Let's get started!

Story: Moving in a new direction

ELLIE RICHMOND

INSURANCE AGENT

Insurance for socially conscious enterprises

www.ellierichmond.ca

Although I'm very content with my career as an insurance agent, one of the personal conflicts I often face is schmoozing with my lawyer clients and competitors in the downtown scene to win business or build relationships. I often feel as though I am swimming upstream, working for the wrong audience.

Rhonda emailed me information about one of her upcoming workshops. Two days before it was to happen, I suddenly felt the urge to take it. I knew her capacity as a branding expert. I've watched the interesting things she's been involved with since I've known her—and I've known her for a very long time. I knew her talent.

By the end of the workshop, I realized that the market I was serving was not suited to my personality. The way in which her workbook is laid out, and how the day flowed, helped me analyze my target market and competition. It became clear that I would be moving in a different direction by serving a new target audience. I knew who I wanted to sell insurance to: socially conscious businesses. Rhonda and I determined that if I concentrated on working with like-minded people there would be a much easier flow with relationships.

Shortly after her workshop, I started implementing action steps right away. It's as if I had a to-do list that included even the simplest things like buying a new filing cabinet and researching opportunities to fund my new branding. But one big action step was getting to know more about my new target group. Rhonda and I created a questionnaire and I went out and interviewed them. I wanted to find out what they needed, their challenges and what is important to them. There was a lot to do before I would be fully armed to service them.

When I was at the stage of developing my business cards, Rhonda introduced me to a graphic designer who works with socially responsible clients. Again, she made sure the designer I worked with was aligned with my purpose. Now I have a business card that is very unique to the insurance business. I'm really going to stand out! Once I develop my website, I'll be ready to market to socially responsible businesses.

I plan on immersing myself in social entrepreneur communities and becoming an example to my prospective target market. My whole way of life will change. I will attend eco-friendly conventions, lectures and volunteer opportunities. The more I'm in their world, the more integrity and respect I'll gain and the more they will get to know me. It's like anything in life; it takes awhile to build someone's trust.

STEP 1

Getting clear on my vision

Step 1: **Getting clear on my vision**

Where I am today

☐ Brand scorecard

☐ How I talk about my offer now

☐ What's working for me

My vision

☐ Why this is important

☐ Visioning exercise

☐ My vision board

Today's date: ....

I will complete this section by: ....

Step 1: **Getting clear on my vision**

WHERE I AM TODAY: Brand Scorecard

Date: ....

1	I do not have a good understanding of how to create a strong brand	1	2	3	4	5	6	7	8	9	10	I have a good understanding of how to create a strong brand
2	I do not have a clear vision for my business	1	2	3	4	5	6	7	8	9	10	I have a clear vision for my business
3	I do not have a written description of my ideal client or customer	1	2	3	4	5	6	7	8	9	10	I have a written description of my ideal client or customer
4	I do not have a list of secondary audiences that I market to regularly	1	2	3	4	5	6	7	8	9	10	I have a list of secondary audiences that I market to regularly
5	My product/service does not stand out from the competition	1	2	3	4	5	6	7	8	9	10	My product/service stands out from the competition
6	I do not know what my clients/customers biggest challenge is right now	1	2	3	4	5	6	7	8	9	10	I know what my clients/customers biggest challenge is right now
7	I do not have an elevator pitch that works for me	1	2	3	4	5	6	7	8	9	10	I have an elevator pitch that works well for me
8	I'm not sure if my marketing materials and website are well designed	1	2	3	4	5	6	7	8	9	10	My marketing materials and website are well designed and aligned to a strong core message
9	I do not have good resources for graphic design and copywriting	1	2	3	4	5	6	7	8	9	10	I have good resources for graphic design and copywriting
10	I do not offer a complete brand experience to my client/customer	1	2	3	4	5	6	7	8	9	10	I offer a complete brand experience to my client/customer
Total	Add column totals											Your score ....

How I talk about my offer now

Spend no more than 5 minutes on this. Just write the way you currently speak about your business. You will see later how far you've come.

I offer ....
(my offer)

to ....,.....to help them
(my ideal client or customer)

.... and ....
(benefit)   *(benefit)*

What makes me different? ....

....

....

Credibility Points: (Why should you trust me?) ....

....

....

What's working for me

It's important to pay attention to what's working for you now and be grateful even if they are small things. Too often we focus on what isn't working. Make it a habit to focus on what is going well each day. This is one of the keys to success.

Inspiration Box

Start a gratitude journal and write what you are grateful for each day. This will move you in a positive direction!

MY VISION

Why this is important

Did you know that Olympic athletes spend a substantial amount of practice time visualizing their success? The **POWER OF VISUALIZATION** has been proven to be extremely successful in helping people reach their goals.

The following exercise will help you achieve clarity about where you are going with your business so you can create a brand that will move you towards your vision and passion.

Visioning exercise

Sit in a quiet and comfortable place. Close your eyes and take a few deep breaths. When you feel relaxed, picture your work life three years from now and how you would like it to be. Picture it in as much detail as possible: a typical day, your environment, the geographical location, who you are with, who your clients or customers are and how much money you are earning. When you have a clear picture, open your eyes and write what you envisioned in the space on the next page.

 To download a recording that will guide you through the visioning exercise go to: www.knowyourdifference.com/freebonus

www.knowyourdifference.com/freebonus

My vision

....

....

....

....

....

....

....

....

....

....

....

....

....

My vision

Look at your vision, and with a red marker, circle three things that give you the most energy and excitement. Write them in the space below.

....

....

....

List three small things you can do to move closer to your vision now. It could be as small as cleaning out your filing cabinet.

....

....

....

Inspiration Box

Look at your vision board every day. Imagine what it will feel like when you have achieved your vision!

My vision board

Create a vision board with images from magazines that represent your vision of the future. Put your board in a place where you can look at it every day and when you look at it imagine how it will feel when you have achieved your vision. This exercise will move you closer to your goals. You don't need to know how, just hold onto that vision.

STEP 2

Getting clear on my ideal client or customer

Step 2: Getting clear on my ideal client or customer

☐ Why this is important
☐ My primary audience
☐ My secondary audience

Today's date: ....

I will complete this section by: ....

Step 2: **Getting clear on my ideal client or customer**

Why this is important

Your ideal client or customer is often called your *primary audience* in marketing lingo. Your primary audience is the one who purchases your product or service directly from you. The more focused you are on who you are talking to, the better your message will be heard. Many of my clients tell me their audience is *everyone* but it cannot be everyone. The following exercises will help you get a better description of your primary audience.

My Primary Audience

There are two parts to this exercise:

Part 1: A written description of your primary audience

Part 2: A visual description of your primary audience

Part 1: A written description of my primary audience

Write a short paragraph that describes your primary audience (on page 34). It should be the group you aspire to serve, which may be different from the group you are currently serving. If you are starting something new, think carefully about whom you want your client or customer to be. Below is an example using **know your** $difference$™.

Primary audience for know your $difference$™

Name: **The passionate entrepreneur**

"My primary audience is the entrepreneur or small business owner who is experienced in the business world and, in many cases, has had a number of different careers. The age group is 40-plus with 15–20 years work experience. They are leaving the corporate world to start a business that is more meaningful and purposeful or they have been in business for many years and are pursuing the goal of moving their business to the next level. Their business is often an innovative product or service, or a social enterprise (doing work for the good of society) and

they are absolutely passionate about it. Here are the words to describe my primary audience: visionary, motivated, creative thinker, energetic, optimistic, pioneers of change, courageous, problem solvers. They are self-aware, into personal development and always want to learn and improve their lives. They often work with a business coach to ensure steady progress.

My offer helps them get focused, get clear on their direction, talk about their business clearly and bring their brand to life in a way that inspires their audience to take action."

Answer the questions below to help you begin to formulate a clear picture of your primary audience.

How old are they? (It may be a wide age range or may not be relevant.)

Where do they live?

What are their core values?

What do they do for a living? (May or may not be relevant.)

What is their economic situation?

What is most important to them?

What is their greatest challenge?

What problem does your product or service solve for them?

Their background or culture may be diverse, but what do they share in common? Try to describe their mindset. Put yourself in their shoes. Close your eyes and picture their life. Jot notes below and on the next page, write a detailed paragraph that describes your primary audience.

....

....

....

My primary audience description:

....

....

....

....

....

....

....

Give a simple descriptive name to your primary audience

Name: ....

Review what you've written about your primary audience and circle the three most important things that stand out. List them below.

....

....

Refer to this list often as you move through this process.

How far apart is the target you've described above from your current client or customer?
Circle the appropriate number (1 = pretty close and 10 = miles away).

1   2   3   4   5   6   7   8   9   10

How far apart is the target you've described above from the target you've been marketing to?
Circle the appropriate number (1 = pretty close and 10 = miles away).

1   2   3   4   5   6   7   8   9   10

If you've answered 6 and above for either question, you need to pay careful attention to who you are marketing to.

Part 2: A visual description of my primary audience

Using your written description, cut images from old magazines and create a collage of your primary audience and paste below with a glue stick. This exercise helps you get a clearer picture of who they are.

MY SECONDARY AUDIENCE

Your secondary audience is just as important. This group is in the position to send clients or customers your way and spread the word for you. In the space below, make a list of the kinds of people who form your secondary audience. For example, a secondary audience for **know your difference**™ would be business coaches. When thinking about your secondary audience, try to come up with as many ideas as you can. Brainstorming with a friend is helpful. Circle your top three.

My secondary audience:

....

....

....

....

....

....

....

It is crucial to keep your primary and secondary audiences in mind in all of your marketing. You may not be marketing to them in the same way.

You now have clarity on your vision and your ideal client or customer. Are you asking yourself one of these common questions?

How can I...
• Get Rhonda's direct input through this process?
• Get group support to work through these steps and have my questions answered?

☞ *To learn about opportunities to accelerate your progress, go to* <u>*www.knowyourdifference.com/breakthrough*</u> *NOW to choose the program that suits you best!*

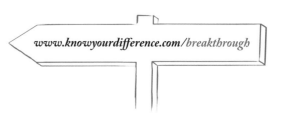

www.knowyourdifference.com/breakthrough

STEP 3
Getting clear on my competition

Step 3: **Getting clear on my competition**

☐ Why this is important
☐ Comparing three competitors
☐ Brand attributes

Today's date: ....

I will complete this section by: ....

know your *difference*™ a branding workbook

Step 3: **Getting clear on my competition**

Why this is important

Before you can differentiate your business, it's important to look at how your competition describes their businesses. Often you will find they all sound the same. You may also find gaps or new opportunities in the market that are not yet filled. In the chart on the following page, list three competitors and how they describe themselves (see the example below).

Comparing my three competitors
know your *difference*™ competition

COMPETITOR'S NAME AND WEBSITE	DESCRIPTION (ABOUT) AND LIST OF SERVICES	WHAT'S THE OVERALL FEELING YOU GET LOOKING AT THE SITE?
Branding Firm "A" strategic brand consulting and design www.brandingfirma.com	Are prospects passing you by? We can help you build your brand to get noticed! We offer: • Brand positioning • Graphic design • Web design • Marketing	Nothing stands out. The things they say are similar to other branding firms. It makes me wonder what their strengths are.

Comparing my three competitors

COMPETITOR'S NAME AND WEBSITE	DESCRIPTION (ABOUT) AND LIST OF SERVICES	WHAT'S THE OVERALL FEELING YOU GET LOOKING AT THE SITE?

know your *difference*™   a branding workbook

When you look at your competition, what patterns are appearing? How can you be different?
Have you discovered any future opportunities in doing this research? Is there a need you can fill?
Write your ideas below.

Brand attributes

Here's another way to see how well you stand out from your competition. On the next page is an example of a competitive study done for **know your** *difference*™. The column on the far left is a list of attributes commonly used by **know your** *difference*™ and its competitors*. Remember, you are looking for ways to talk about your business that makes you different from your competition. The areas highlighted in gray are opportunities for **know your** *difference*™ to talk about the business in a different way.

*The names of **know your** *difference*™ *competitors have been omitted to protect their image and identity.*

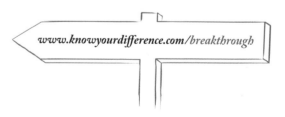

www.knowyourdifference.com/breakthrough

know your *difference*™   a branding workbook

BRAND ATTRIBUTES OR PHRASES USED TO DESCRIBE THE BUSINESS	COMPETITOR A	COMPETITOR B	COMPETITOR C	know your difference™
PROVEN APPROACH	✕	✕	✕	
STRATEGIC	✕	✕		
INCREASE YOUR BRAND VALUE	✕	✕	✕	
EXCELLENT SERVICE	✕	✕	✕	
FIND YOUR USP	✕	✕	✕	
BRAND POSITIONING STRATEGY	✕	✕	✕	
DIFFERENTIATION	✕	✕	✕	✕
ATTRACT MORE BUSINESS	✕	✕	✕	✕
IMPROVE YOUR ROI	✕	✕	✕	
COMBINATION OF BRANDING PRINCIPLES AND PERSONAL DEVELOPMENT				✕
COST EFFECTIVE FOR THE ENTREPRENEUR OR SMALL BUSINESS				✕
UNIQUE BUSINESS MODEL FOR THE BRANDING INDUSTRY				✕

The three phrases that are unique to know your difference™ **are:**

1. *The combination of branding principles and personal development.*
2. *Cost effective for the entrepreneur or small business owner.*
3. *A unique business model for the branding industry.*

My brand attributes

Using the table below, write the names of your three competitors at the top of each column and your brand name in the far right column. In the left-hand column, make a list of brand attributes or phrases that each competitor uses to describe their product or service (check their website for the words and phrases they use). Do the same for your offer, adding as many attributes or phrases as you like. Then, put an x in each column to see which attributes are commonly used by you and your competitors. Here is a perfect opportunity to see if the way you market your offer is similar to or different from your competition.

BRAND ATTRIBUTES OR PHRASES USED TO DESCRIBE THE BUSINESS	COMPETITOR 1	COMPETITOR 2	COMPETITOR 3	MY BUSINESS

When you look at your competition, what words or phrases are not being used by them?
Write three below:

....

....

....

know your *difference*™   **a branding workbook**

STEP 4
Getting insights

Step 4: **Getting insights**

Self interview

☐ Why this is important

☐ Instructions

☐ Self interview questions

Insight interviews

☐ Why this is important

☐ Instructions

☐ Interview schedule

☐ Questions

☐ Interview notes

☐ Most important insights

☐ Interview keywords

Turning your differentiator into benefits

Today's date: ....

I will complete this section by: ....

Note: You will need more time for this section. Allow at least two weeks.

SELF INTERVIEW

Why this is important

It will become clear why you are doing what you do. As you go through this process, it will bring up other important questions to ponder about your business.

Instructions

Ask a friend to interview you about your business, using the questions provided on the next page. Feel free to add your own questions. Try to get as much information as you can in the areas of strengths, positive attributes and uniqueness and how your product or service demonstrates those qualities. Have your interviewer take detailed notes on the pages provided. You will refer to the notes later on. Please make sure he or she writes legibly so you can read and understand the notes afterwards.

Inspiration **Box**

"Clarity is power."

—*BUCKMINSTER FULLER*

Self interview questions

1. What do you offer? Is it different from your future vision?

....

....

....

2. Why do you do what you do?

....

....

....

3. What led you to do this work? What were you doing before?

....

....

....

4. What skills or unique education do you have that others in your industry don't and how do your clients or customers benefit from this?

....

....

....

know your *difference*™   **a branding workbook**

5. What makes you credible with the product or service you offer? List as many things as you can.

....

....

....

6. What is the best result you can give your client or customer?

....

....

....

7. How is your product or service different from the competition?

....

....

....

8. What is your greatest accomplishment in your work?

....

....

....

9. What is the best thing about your product or service?

....

....

....

10. Is your product or service the *only* of anything?

....

....

....

Self interview notes and observations:

....

....

....

....

....

....

After your self interview, review your notes and pull out key words as follows:

1. Use a **GREEN** marker to circle words or phrases that describe what you **OFFER.**
2. Use a **BLUE** marker to circle words or phrases that make you **CREDIBLE** (unique skills, experience, education).
3. Use a **RED** marker to circle things that make you **DIFFERENT** from others.

Please do this immediately following your interview while it is still fresh.

List your key words below

green (offer descriptions)	blue (credibility points)	red (differentiators)
....	....	....
....	....	....
....	....	....
....	....	....
....	....	....
....	....	....

INSIGHT INTERVIEWS

Why this is important
Insight interviews will help you create a differentiated brand by having conversations with your client
or customer. They can be current, past or even prospects. This process can also be used as a business development
tool to reconnect with clients or customers who have not been active for some time.

When you ask people for honest feedback, it's amazing what they will tell you. Being asked is usually taken as a
compliment. I have gone through this exercise many times for my corporate clients.

To begin, I create a list of questions that I use as conversation starters. Interviews are scheduled in advance
and are done over the phone, and in some cases, I make calls all over the world! Over the
years, I've honed the questions to create a general list, which I then customize for each client. Through these inter-
views, I discover the most amazing things for my clients: products and services their
customers want, ideas for acquiring new business, constructive feedback on things they could improve upon, new
revenue sources and pricing models and even new markets to pursue! I recommend that
you do at least five interviews, but set a goal for 10*. This is valuable market research for you!

 * To listen to a recording with more information on Insight Interviews go to:
www.knowyourdifference.com/freebonus

www.knowyourdifference.com/freebonus

Please review the instructions carefully before you start.

Instructions

Interview a variety of people. If possible, include current clients or customers, past clients, as well as prospects. Try to include people from your primary and secondary audiences. You can do the interview on the phone or in person. I've given you space for 10 interviews, but you decide on the number of interviews that feel right for you. (I recommend a minimum of five.)

Here are a few examples of potential interviewees:
- A past or current client or customer
- An ideal client, customer or prospect (someone you would love to be your client but isn't yet)

- If you are selling a product, interview people who have purchased your product, the retailer that carries your product, or the distributor who provided your product to the retailer
- If your product or service is not launched yet, interview a potential customer
- A supplier

Tip: I always ask permission to tape record the conversations so that I can go back later and listen for more insights and make notes. I usually receive a positive response. I find that it is never an imposition, because people love to help and give feedback.

Inspiration Box

"You have nothing to lose and everything to gain by asking."

—*JACK CANFIELD*

What you will need
Three markers: **RED, BLUE, GREEN**
Optional: a digital recorder

The set up
Call or e-mail each person and **SCHEDULE** a time
to talk. You can say something like, *"I'm working
on getting insights for my business and I'd like
to ask you a few questions. It should take about
fifteen minutes."*

*Note: These interviews must be done in a
conversation. The conversation is what gives you
the insights. Use the following page to create
a schedule.*

Interview schedule

Name .... Date/time ....

Name .... Date/time ....

Name .... Date/time ....

Name .... Date/time ....

Name .... Date/time ....

Name .... Date/time ....

Name .... Date/time ....

Name .... Date/time ....

Name .... Date/time ....

Name .... Date/time ....

Be careful not to book your interviews too close to together or try to do too many on the same day.
Give yourself an hour timeslot for each interview so you can review your notes after the call and record
your key insights while they are fresh.

Do you have questions about your business model? Your pricing? Your name or tagline? Here's your chance to get great feedback.

Interview questions

The questions provided are **CONVERSATION STARTERS**. Feel free to add your own. Try to get as much information as you can in the areas of strengths, positive attributes and uniqueness, and how your product or service demonstrates those qualities. You can create separate questions for prospects that have not yet used your product or service. Record both the positive and the negative feedback. (Negative information is just as valuable. Use it to improve your product or service.) It's a good idea to email the questions in advance to give the interviewee an opportunity to think about them. Make sure to have the conversation in real time: on the phone, through Skype or in person.

If you have some ideas that you'd like to test out, this is your opportunity. For example, if you are wondering what to charge for a membership or workshop, if you have questions about your business model or your pricing, or if you'd like to test

out a name or tagline, you can formulate questions and add them to your list.

These questions are conversation starters. You don't need to stick exactly to the format. It's all about getting insights to help you grow your business.

Make sure to take good notes and write neatly. You will be referring back to these notes as part of the process. Follow the post-interview instructions. You may be on a call for 15 minutes but give yourself an hour to make notes and record key insights.

Your notes and recording the information
Take detailed notes, using the pages provided in the workbook. You will refer to the notes later; write neatly to ensure you can read what you wrote.

Interview questions

Go through the questions and think about what you can add that is specific to your offer. The questions will vary, depending on who you are talking to: past client or customer, current or prospective.

1. *How would you describe my product/service?*
2. *How did you hear about my product/service and what gave you the confidence to buy?*
3. *How would you rate your experience with my product/service, using a scale of one to ten (delve deeper by asking why they chose the number they did)? What can be improved?*
4. *What is the main problem or challenge my product/service solves for you?*
5. *What is the greatest benefit of using my product/service and why?*
6. *What options were you considering and what made you choose my product/service?*
7. *Is there another need I can fill for you?*
8. *Where do you think my industry is headed? (This is an opportunity to anticipate or prepare for future needs.)*
9. *Who do you think can benefit most from my product/service?*
10. *How would you prefer to receive updates and information from me? (How would you like me to market to you?)*

Other questions you'd like to ask:

....

....

....

....

....

If you have some ideas that you'd like to test out, this is your opportunity. For example, if you are wondering what to charge for a membership or workshop, if you have questions about your business model or your pricing, or if you'd like to test out a name or tagline, you can formulate questions and add them to your list.

1. How would you describe my product/service?

....

....

....

....

Interview #1

Name ....

Date ....

2. How did you hear about my product/service and what gave you the confidence to buy?

....

....

....

....

3. How would you rate your experience with my product/service, using a scale of one to ten (delve deeper by asking why they chose the number they did)? What can be improved?

....

....

....

....

4.   What is the main problem or challenge my product/service solves for you?

....

....

....

....

5.   What is the greatest benefit of using my product/service and why?

....

....

....

....

6.   What options were you considering and what made you choose my product/service?

....

....

....

....

Interview #1 continued

7. Is there another need I can fill for you?

....

....

....

....

8. Where do you think my industry is headed?
   (This is an opportunity to anticipate or prepare for future needs.)

....

....

....

....

9. Who do you think can benefit most from my product/service?

....

....

....

....

10. How would you prefer to receive updates and information from me?
    (How would you like me to market to you?)

....

....

....

....

Responses to other questions:

....

....

....

....

....

....

....

....

Interview #1 continued

Review your notes from this interview and pull out key words as follows:

1. Use a **GREEN** marker to circle words or phrases that describe what you **OFFER.**
2. Use a **BLUE** marker to circle words or phrases that make you **CREDIBLE** (unique skills, experience, education).
3. Use a **RED** marker to circle things that make you **DIFFERENT** from others.

Please do this immediately following your interview while it is still fresh.

List your key words below

green (offer descriptions)	blue (credibility points)	red (differentiators)
....	....	....
....	....	....
....	....	....
....	....	....
....	....	....
....	....	....

know your *difference*™ a branding workbook

What are your three main insights from this interview? Put an asterisk beside the most important one.

1 ....

....

....

2 ....

....

....

3 ....

....

....

www.knowyourdifference.com/breakthrough

1. How would you describe my product/service?

....

....

....

....

....

Interview #2

Name ....

Date ....

2. How did you hear about my product/service and what gave you the confidence to buy?

....

....

....

....

3. How would you rate your experience with my product/service, using a scale of one to ten (delve deeper by asking why they chose the number they did). What can be improved?

....

....

....

....

4. What is the main problem or challenge my product/service solves for you?

....

....

....

....

5. What is the greatest benefit of using my product/service and why?

....

....

....

....

6. What options were you considering and what made you choose my product/service?

....

....

....

....

Interview #2 continued

7. Is there another need I can fill for you?

....

....

....

....

8. Where do you think my industry is headed?
    (This is an opportunity to anticipate or prepare for future needs.)

....

....

....

....

9. Who do you think can benefit most from my product/service?

....

....

....

....

know your di*ff*erence™ a branding workbook

10. How would you prefer to receive updates and information from me?
(How would you like me to market to you?)

....

....

....

....

Responses to other questions:

....

....

....

....

....

....

....

....

Review your notes from this interview and pull out key words as follows:

1. Use a **GREEN** marker to circle words or phrases that describe what you **OFFER.**

2. Use a **BLUE** marker to circle words or phrases that make you **CREDIBLE** (unique skills, experience, education).

Interview #2 continued

3. Use a **RED** marker to circle things that make you **DIFFERENT** from others.

Please do this immediately following your interview while it is still fresh.

List your key words below

green (offer descriptions)	blue (credibility points)	red (differentiators)

What are your three main insights from this interview? Put an asterisk beside the most important one.

1 ....

....

....

2 ....

....

....

3 ....

....

....

www.knowyourdifference.com/breakthrough

1. How would you describe my product/service?

Interview #3

Name ....

Date ....

2. How did you hear about my product/service and what gave you the confidence to buy?

3. How would you rate your experience with my product/service, using a scale of one to ten (delve deeper by asking why they chose the number they did). What can be improved?

4. What is the main problem or challenge my product/service solves for you?

5. What is the greatest benefit of using my product/service and why?

6. What options were you considering and what made you choose my product/service?

Interview #3 continued

7. Is there another need I can fill for you?

....

....

....

....

8. Where do you think my industry is headed?
   (This is an opportunity to anticipate or prepare for future needs.)

....

....

....

9. Who do you think can benefit most from my product/service?

....

....

....

....

10. How would you prefer to receive updates and information from me?
    (How would you like me to market to you?)

....

....

....

....

Responses to other questions:

....

....

....

....

....

....

....

....

Interview #3 continued

Review your notes from this interview and pull out key words as follows:

1. Use a **GREEN** marker to circle words or phrases that describe what you **OFFER.**
2. Use a **BLUE** marker to circle words or phrases that make you **CREDIBLE** (unique skills, experience, education).
3. Use a **RED** marker to circle things that make you **DIFFERENT** from others.

Please do this immediately following your interview while it is still fresh.

List your key words below

green (offer descriptions)	blue (credibility points)	red (differentiators)

What are your three main insights from this interview? Put an asterisk beside the most important one.

1 ....

....

....

2 ....

....

....

3 ....

....

....

www.knowyourdifference.com/breakthrough

Interview #4

Name ....

Date ....

1. How would you describe my product/service?

....

....

....

2. How did you hear about my product/service and what gave you the confidence to buy?

....

....

....

....

3. How would you rate your experience with my product/service, using a scale of one to ten (delve deeper by asking why they chose the number they did). What can be improved?

....

....

....

know your di*fference*™ a branding workbook

4. What is the main problem or challenge my product/service solves for you?

....

....

....

....

5. What is the greatest benefit of using my product/service and why?

....

....

....

....

6. What options were you considering and what made you choose my product/service?

....

....

....

....

7. Is there another need I can fill for you?

Interview #4 continued

....

....

....

....

8. Where do you think my industry is headed?
   (This is an opportunity to anticipate or prepare for future needs.)

....

....

....

....

9. Who do you think can benefit most from my product/service?

....

....

....

....

10. How would you prefer to receive updates and information from me?
    (How would you like me to market to you?)

....

....

....

....

Responses to other questions:

....

....

....

....

....

....

....

....

Interview #4 continued

Review your notes from this interview and pull out key words as follows:

1. Use a **GREEN** marker to circle words or phrases that describe what you **OFFER.**

2. Use a **BLUE** marker to circle words or phrases that make you **CREDIBLE** (unique skills, experience, education).

3. Use a **RED** marker to circle things that make you **DIFFERENT** from others.

Please do this immediately following your interview while it is still fresh.

List your key words below

green (offer descriptions)	blue (credibility points)	red (differentiators)

know your di*ff*erence™   a branding workbook

What are your three main insights from this interview? Put an asterisk beside the most important one.

1 ....

....

....

2 ....

....

....

3 ....

....

....

www.knowyourdifference.com/breakthrough

Interview #5

Name ....

Date ....

1. How would you describe my product/service?

    ....

    ....

    ....

    ....

2. How did you hear about my product/service and what gave you the confidence to buy?

    ....

    ....

    ....

    ....

3. How would you rate your experience with my product/service, using a scale of one to ten (delve deeper by asking why they chose the number they did). What can be improved?

    ....

    ....

    ....

    ....

4. What is the main problem or challenge my product/service solves for you?

....

....

....

....

5. What is the greatest benefit of using my product/service and why?

....

....

....

....

6. What options were you considering and what made you choose my product/service?

....

....

....

....

7. Is there another need I can fill for you?

....

....

....

....

Interview #5 continued

8. Where do you think my industry is headed?
   (This is an opportunity to anticipate or prepare for future needs.)

....

....

....

....

9. Who do you think can benefit most from my product/service?

....

....

....

....

10. How would you prefer to receive updates and information from me?
    (How would you like me to market to you?)

....

....

....

....

Responses to other questions:

....

....

....

....

....

....

....

....

....

Interview #5 continued

Review your notes from this interview and pull out key words as follows:

1. Use a **GREEN** marker to circle words or phrases that describe what you **OFFER.**
2. Use a **BLUE** marker to circle words or phrases that make you **CREDIBLE** (unique skills, experience, education).
3. Use a **RED** marker to circle things that make you **DIFFERENT** from others.

Please do this immediately following your interview while it is still fresh.

List your key words below

green (offer descriptions)	blue (credibility points)	red (differentiators)

What are your three main insights from this interview? Put an asterisk beside the most important one.

1 ....

....

....

2 ....

....

....

3 ....

....

....

www.knowyourdifference.com/breakthrough

Interview #6

Name ....

Date ....

1. How would you describe my product/service?

....

....

....

....

2. How did you hear about my product/service and what gave you the confidence to buy?

....

....

....

....

3. How would you rate your experience with my product/service, using a scale of one to ten (delve deeper by asking why they chose the number they did). What can be improved?

....

....

....

....

4. What is the main problem or challenge my product/service solves for you?

....

....

....

....

5. What is the greatest benefit of using my product/service and why?

....

....

....

....

6. What options were you considering and what made you choose my product/service?

....

....

....

....

7. Is there another need I can fill for you?

Interview #6 continued

....

....

....

....

8. Where do you think my industry is headed?
    (This is an opportunity to anticipate or prepare for future needs.)

....

....

....

....

9. Who do you think can benefit most from my product/service?

....

....

....

....

10. How would you prefer to receive updates and information from me?
    (How would you like me to market to you?)

....

....

....

....

Responses to other questions:

....

....

....

....

....

....

....

....

Review your notes from this interview and pull out key words as follows:

1. Use a **GREEN** marker to circle words or phrases that describe what you **OFFER.**

2. Use a **BLUE** marker to circle words or phrases that make you **CREDIBLE** (unique skills, experience, education).

Interview #6 continued

3. Use a **RED** marker to circle things that make you **DIFFERENT** from others.

Please do this immediately following your interview while it is still fresh.

List your key words below

green (offer descriptions)	blue (credibility points)	red (differentiators)

What are your three main insights from this interview? Put an asterisk beside the most important one.

1 ....

....

....

2 ....

....

....

3 ....

....

....

www.knowyourdifference.com/breakthrough

Interview #7

Name ....

Date ....

1. How would you describe my product/service?

    ....

    ....

    ....

    ....

2. How did you hear about my product/service and what gave you the confidence to buy?

    ....

    ....

    ....

3. How would you rate your experience with my product/service, using a scale of one to ten
    (delve deeper by asking why they chose the number they did). What can be improved?

    ....

    ....

    ....

4. What is the main problem or challenge my product/service solves for you?

....

....

....

....

5. What is the greatest benefit of using my product/service and why?

....

....

....

....

6. What options were you considering and what made you choose my product/service?

....

....

....

....

Interview #7 continued

7. Is there another need I can fill for you?

....

....

....

....

8. Where do you think my industry is headed?
(This is an opportunity to anticipate or prepare for future needs.)

....

....

....

....

9. Who do you think can benefit most from my product/service?

....

....

....

....

10. How would you prefer to receive updates and information from me?
    (How would you like me to market to you?)

....

....

....

....

Responses to other questions:

....

....

....

....

....

....

....

....

Interview #7 continued

Review your notes from this interview and pull out key words as follows:

1. Use a **GREEN** marker to circle words or phrases that describe what you **OFFER.**

2. Use a **BLUE** marker to circle words or phrases that make you **CREDIBLE** (unique skills, experience, education).

3. Use a **RED** marker to circle things that make you **DIFFERENT** from others.

Please do this immediately following your interview while it is still fresh.

List your key words below

green (offer descriptions)	blue (credibility points)	red (differentiators)
....	....	....
....	....	....
....	....	....
....	....	....
....	....	....
....	....	....

know your *difference*™ a branding workbook

What are your three main insights from this interview? Put an asterisk beside the most important one.

1 ....

....

....

2 ....

....

....

3 ....

....

....

www.knowyourdifference.com/breakthrough

1. How would you describe my product/service?

....

....

....

....

Interview #8

Name ....

Date ....

2. How did you hear about my product/service and what gave you the confidence to buy?

....

....

....

....

3. How would you rate your experience with my product/service, using a scale of one to ten (delve deeper by asking why they chose the number they did). What can be improved?

....

....

....

....

4. What is the main problem or challenge my product/service solves for you?

....

....

....

....

5. What is the greatest benefit of using my product/service and why?

....

....

....

....

6. What options were you considering and what made you choose my product/service?

....

....

....

....

7. Is there another need I can fill for you?

Interview #8 continued

....

....

....

....

8. Where do you think my industry is headed?
    (This is an opportunity to anticipate or prepare for future needs.)

....

....

....

....

9. Who do you think can benefit most from my product/service?

....

....

....

....

10. How would you prefer to receive updates and information from me?
(How would you like me to market to you?)

....

....

....

....

Responses to other questions:

....

....

....

....

....

....

....

....

Review your notes from this interview and pull out key words as follows:

1. Use a **GREEN** marker to circle words or phrases that describe what you **OFFER.**

2. Use a **BLUE** marker to circle words or phrases that make you **CREDIBLE** (unique skills, experience, education).

Interview #8 continued

3. Use a **RED** marker to circle things that make you **DIFFERENT** from others.

Please do this immediately following your interview while it is still fresh.

List your key words below

green (offer descriptions)	blue (credibility points)	red (differentiators)
....	....	....
....	....	....
....	....	....
....	....	....
....	....	....
....	....	....

What are your three main insights from this interview? Put an asterisk beside the most important one.

1 ....

....

....

2 ....

....

....

3 ....

....

....

www.knowyourdifference.com/breakthrough

Interview #9

Name ....

Date ....

1.   How would you describe my product/service?

....

....

....

2.   How did you hear about my product/service and what gave you the confidence to buy?

....

....

....

....

3.   How would you rate your experience with my product/service, using a scale of one to ten (delve deeper by asking why they chose the number they did). What can be improved?

....

....

....

....

4. What is the main problem or challenge my product/service solves for you?

....

....

....

....

5. What is the greatest benefit of using my product/service and why?

....

....

....

....

6. What options were you considering and what made you choose my product/service?

....

....

....

....

7. Is there another need I can fill for you?

....

Interview #9 continued

....

....

....

8. Where do you think my industry is headed?
    (This is an opportunity to anticipate or prepare for future needs.)

....

....

....

....

9. Who do you think can benefit most from my product/service?

....

....

....

....

know your difference™ **a branding workbook**

10. How would you prefer to receive updates and information from me?
    (How would you like me to market to you?)

....

....

....

....

Responses to other questions:

....

....

....

....

....

....

....

....

Review your notes from this interview and pull out key words as follows:

1. Use a **GREEN** marker to circle words or phrases that describe what you **OFFER.**

2. Use a **BLUE** marker to circle words or phrases that make you **CREDIBLE** (unique skills, experience, education).

Interview #9 continued

3. Use a **RED** marker to circle things that make you **DIFFERENT** from others.

Please do this immediately following your interview while it is still fresh.

List your key words below

green (offer descriptions)	blue (credibility points)	red (differentiators)
....	....	....
....	....	....
....	....	....
....	....	....
....	....	....
....	....	....

What are your three main insights from this interview? Put an asterisk beside the most important one.

1 ....

....

....

2 ....

....

....

3 ....

....

....

www.knowyourdifference.com/breakthrough

Interview #10

Name ....

Date ....

1. How would you describe my product/service?

    ....

    ....

    ....

    ....

2. How did you hear about my product/service and what gave you the confidence to buy?

    ....

    ....

    ....

    ....

3. How would you rate your experience with my product/service, using a scale of one to ten
    (delve deeper by asking why they chose the number they did). What can be improved?

    ....

    ....

    ....

    ....

4. What is the main problem or challenge my product/service solves for you?

....

....

....

....

5. What is the greatest benefit of using my product/service and why?

....

....

....

....

6. What options were you considering and what made you choose my product/service?

....

....

....

....

Interview #10 continued

7. Is there another need I can fill for you?

....

....

....

....

8. Where do you think my industry is headed?
    (This is an opportunity to anticipate or prepare for future needs.)

....

....

....

....

9. Who do you think can benefit most from my product/service?

....

....

....

10. How would you prefer to receive updates and information from me?
(How would you like me to market to you?)

....

....

....

....

Responses to other questions:

....

....

....

....

....

....

....

....

Review your notes from this interview and pull out key words as follows:

1. Use a **GREEN** marker to circle words or phrases that describe what you **OFFER.**

2. Use a **BLUE** marker to circle words or phrases that make you **CREDIBLE** (unique skills, experience, education).

Interview #10 continued

3. Use a **RED** marker to circle things that make you **DIFFERENT** from others.

Please do this immediately following your interview while it is still fresh.

List your key words below

green (offer descriptions)	blue (credibility points)	red (differentiators)

☞ *To listen to a recording that will help you choose your key words go to:* *www.knowyourdifference.com/freebonus*

What are your three main insights from this interview? Put an asterisk beside the most important one.

1 ....

....

....

2 ....

....

....

3 ....

....

....

www.knowyourdifference.com/freebonus

Most important insights

There are two parts to completing the Insight interview process:

1.   *Take note of your main insights and create related action steps.*
2.   *Review your lists of key words and choose the best ones to describe your brand.*

List your 10 main insights from all of your interviews below and put asterisks
beside the three most important overall insights.

1 ....

2 ....

3 ....

4 ....

5 ....

6 ....

7 ....

8 ....

9 ....

10 ....

Using the chart below, list your three main insights from the previous page and three action steps you are going to take to move your business forward.

INSIGHT	ACTION STEP
EXAMPLE: some know your difference™ clients think of themselves as entrepreneurs while others think of themselves as solopreneurs.	Do further research. Decide which word best describes know your difference™ primary audience. Get the language right.

Interview key words

Follow these instructions very carefully!

1. Upon completion of all of your interviews, review your key words and list all of them below in the appropriate columns.
2. Review each column and circle the **THREE** most important key words from each.
3. Look at the green list and put an asterisk beside the **ONE** thing that best describes your offer.
4. Look at the blue list – it should already have the **THREE** things that make you most credible circled.
5. Then look at the red list and put an asterisk beside the **ONE** biggest differentiator.

green (offer descriptions)   blue (credibility points)   red (differentiators)

know your *difference*™   a branding workbook

Turning your differentiator into benefits

Now that you've chosen the ONE biggest differentiator (from the interview keywords on page 122), or one thing that makes you most unique, write it in the left hand column. In the right hand column, write as many things you can think of that are benefits to your differentiator. Number them in order of importance and write the top two below.

Note: If you can't come up with a list of benefits, you've chosen the wrong differentiator. Go back and review your list on page 122.

MY BIGGEST DIFFERENTIATOR	BENEFITS TO MY CLIENT OR CUSTOMER
Example: combination of branding principles and personal development tools	Example: ensures they are clear and passionate about their brand

Benefit #1 ....

Benefit #2 ....

You have now completed the first 4 steps! Are you asking yourself one of these common questions?

How can I…
- Get Rhonda's direct input through this process?
- Get group support to work through these steps and have my questions answered?

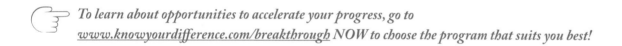 *To learn about opportunities to accelerate your progress, go to www.knowyourdifference.com/breakthrough NOW to choose the program that suits you best!*

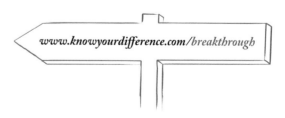

www.knowyourdifference.com/breakthrough

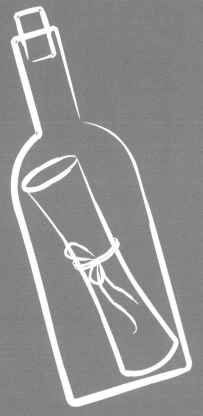

STEP 5
Developing my differentiated message

Step 5: **Developing my differentiated message**

☐ Why this is important
☐ Putting together your difference statement
☐ Getting feedback
☐ My elevator pitch

Today's date: ....

I will complete this section by: ....

know your *difference*™ a branding workbook

Step 5: **Developing my differentiated message**

Why this is important

This is where the rubber meets the road. In this section, you will use all the previous components in the workbook to put together a statement that describes what you do, for whom, the benefits, why you are different and what makes you a credible source.

Putting together your difference statement

This is the same statement you filled in on Page 24 of this workbook, but don't peek! I want you to see how far you've come. Fill this in based on your new information and then go back and compare.

I offer ....
(my offer from page 122)

to ....
(name of my primary audience from page 34)

to help them .... and ....
(benefit #1 from page 123)   *(benefit #2 from page 123)*

What makes me different? (list Three circled differentiators from page 122)

....

....

....

Credibility points (Why you should trust me from page 122)

....

....

....

You can go back to page 24 and compare this to the statement you filled in at the beginning.
You should see a big improvement!

know your *difference*™   a branding workbook

Finessing your statement

Your statement will need some finessing; however, you should be much closer to a differentiated message compared to where you started. You may want to involve a copywriter to help you with this process. If you don't have the budget at this point, contact a communications or journalism student. Keep fine-tuning your message until you are happy with it.

Go back to your competition on page 46 and the three new words you found that are different. See if you can incorporate these into your statement. Make sure that you sound different from your competition.

In marketing lingo, this is your brand positioning statement. It is for internal use to guide your business but it will set the stage for your marketing. You can evolve it into your "elevator pitch." Once you get your statement sounding the way that you like, it will set the stage for all of your future business activities. Whenever you need to make a business decision, go back to this statement and ask yourself if it's aligned.

Getting feedback

It's a good idea to test your refined statement and see how well it resonates with people. Here are questions you can ask to get feedback:

1. *From what you know about my business, how well do you think my statement describes the value of what I provide? Rate it on a scale of 1 to 10 (1 = needs a lot of work and 10 = it's bang on, you've nailed it!)*
2. *What changes would you make?*
3. *Do you have any other feedback?*

When you feel good about your difference statement, you are ready to move forward and bring your brand to life!

My elevator pitch

Evolve your difference statement into an "elevator pitch." The term "elevator pitch" refers to the idea that it should be possible to tell someone clearly what you do in the same amount of time as an elevator ride (approximately 30 seconds to 2 minutes). Make sure it flows easily when you say it. The written word is quite different from the spoken word. Practice saying it in front of a mirror before you go to an event.

If you deliver your statement well, people will want to know more. This is where you tie in your 3 top differentiators and credibility points. The more authentic and real your story is, the better.

Here's my elevator pitch for **know your difference**™

"I help entrepreneurs and small business owners get clear on how they are different from their competition so they can market themselves more effectively. I have 20 years experience in helping global brands differentiate."

I usually get asked for my card before I can finish! When they want to know more, I tell the story of the unique business model I've created and how the business started out of a need to help friends struggling during the recession. The story is authentic and interesting to people!

This takes a lot of practice and it will evolve and change. It took me a while to nail it. You will know when its working for you!

The term "elevator pitch" refers to the idea that it should be possible to tell someone clearly what you do in the same amount of time as an elevator ride.

STEP 6
Bringing my brand to life

Step 6: Bringing my brand to life

My marketing toolbox
☐ Why this is important

Branded experiences
☐ How I want my clients or customers to feel

Branded Inspiration
☐ Why this is important
☐ Brand personality
☐ Brand values
☐ Brand imagery
☐ Testing your brand alignment
☐ Brand Summary

Inside Design
☐ Why this is important
☐ Choosing the right graphic designer
☐ How to find a graphic designer
☐ Pricing design work
☐ The process of working with a designer
☐ Evaluating design work that is presented to you
☐ Giving your designer feedback

Inside writing
☐ Why this is important
☐ Naming your brand

Get the word out!
☐ Why this is important
☐ Networking events
☐ Online marketing
☐ Social media
☐ YouTube

Today's date: ....

I will complete this section by: ....

Step 6: **Bringing my brand to life**

CONGRATULATIONS! You've done the heavy lifting. It is time to take your difference statement and use it as a foundation to bring your brand to life.

The key to building a strong brand is to first develop a clear and compelling point of difference that speaks to your audience, then bring your brand to life by creating consistent marketing tools and branded experiences that are aligned with your point of difference. You have now developed your clear point of difference and you are ready to create your marketing toolbox. Once this is done, you can start to think about getting the word out!

MY MARKETING TOOLBOX

Why this is important

Marketing tools are the things you can use to express your brand and get noticed; for example, your website. Marketing has dramatically changed over the past 10 years and there are lots of new tools available to entrepreneurs and small business owners. Here's a list of tools commonly used today:

- Logo
- Business cards
- Website
- Blog
- E-newsletter
- Social media, such as LinkedIn, Twitter and Facebook and YouTube

Today, there is less focus on printed materials, such as brochures and more on electronic media. There are good books and people that can help you in this area. I have recommended some reading materials at the end of the workbook for you to consider. For the web alone, there is a whole science behind marketing your business and this can be overwhelming. If you need help, ask for it!

Your marketing should be a planned and well thought-out strategy. **DON'T FORGET TO KEEP GOING BACK TO YOUR PRIMARY AND SECONDARY AUDIENCES!**

In all your marketing, consistency is key. Make sure you hire a good and experienced graphic designer. He or she will help you not only develop your logo and the visual style for your website and marketing materials, but ensure that all the components of your marketing tools have a consistent look and feel. (If your budget is tight, go to your local art college and hire a graphic design student.) I will explain more about how to hire the right designer for your project later on in the workbook.

BRANDED EXPERIENCES

How I want my client or customer to feel

How would you like your client or customer to feel after working with you or using your product?

Circle the **TOP 10**, narrow the list to the **TOP THREE**, and finally, pick your **NUMBER ONE**.

Able	*Authentic*	*Committed*	*Evolved*	*Interested*	*Refreshed*
Accepting	*Awed*	*Confident*	*Excited*	*Intrigued*	*Rejuvenated*
Accountable	*Beautiful*	*Content*	*Expectant*	*Invigorated*	*Relaxed*
Adventurous	*Blissful*	*Curious*	*Fascinated*	*Mindful*	*Rested*
Alert	*Brave*	*Elated*	*Fulfilled*	*Open*	*Restored*
Alive	*Bubbly*	*Empowered*	*Generous*	*Optimistic*	*Safe*
Amazed	*Calm*	*Energetic*	*Gracious*	*Passionate*	*Secure*
Amused	*Centered*	*Engaged*	*Happy*	*Pleased*	*Tranquil*
Animated	*Clear headed*	*Engrossed*	*Healthy*	*Proud*	*Trusting*
Ardent	*Clarity*	*Enthralled*	*Helpful*	*Purposeful*	*Warm*
Astonished	*Comfort*	*Enthused*	*Inspired*	*Radiant*	*Wonderful*

The feeling I want my client/customer to walk away with is: ....

Differentiate with branded experiences

Align your business to your brand by creating *branded experiences.* Every interaction your client or customer has with your brand—from the look of your business card to your customer service—makes a lasting impression about who you are and how you do business.

Customers don't just use your products or services, they *experience* your brand. To the utmost extent possible, you want to control those events to ensure that your client or customer has an experience that is consistent with your brand message. In other words, you need to *walk your talk.*

know your difference™ brand is about giving clarity to people. *"Clarity"* is the feeling I want my clients to walk away with. I make sure to host my workshops at inspiring and quiet venues where people will be able to think clearly. I have been to enough events in dark conference centers with bad lighting, bad food and distractions to understand the potential impact of venue.

Now that you have chosen the *feeling* you want your customers to walk away with, are there any changes you can make on how you deliver your offer? How will you ensure the customer has an experience that is consistent with that feeling?

Let's say for example, that your feeling word is, *"calm."*

Ask yourself, *"How does 'calm' translate into my customers' experiences, as it relates to…"*
• The way they access information about my product or service: Is it easy to access and understand?
• The way they buy from me: Is the process stressful or effortless?
• The way my product is packaged: Is it one of those packages that is difficult to open?

List three things you can do to create a branded experience for your client or customer.

1 ....

2 ....

3 ....

BRAND INSPIRATION

Why this is important

The next exercises will help you begin to create a mental picture of how your brand will come to life.

This will be important information to feed your creative team.

Brand Personality

If you had to describe your brand's personality, what words would you choose to describe it?

Choose 10 words and then narrow them to three.

Active	Creative	Enterprising	Gracious	Joyful	Relationship oriented
Adaptable	Curious	Enthusiastic	Green	Jubilant	Relaxed
Adventurous	Dependable	Ethical	Helpful	Knowledgeable	Reliable
Appreciative	Detailed	Expressive	Holistic	Mellow	Sincere
Attentive	Determined	Forgiving	Humble	Motivating	Socially responsible
Bold	Diplomatic	Friendly	Humorous	Nurturing	Stable/long-standing
Careful	Disciplined	Fun	Imaginative	Open	Steadfast
Caring	Discreet	Game changer	Independent	Optimistic	Supportive
Centered	Dynamic	Generous	Industrious	Over delivering	Team building
Competent	Efficient	Gentle	Innovative	Polite	Tranquil
Competitive	Empowering	Genuine	Intellectual	Positive	Trusted advisor
Confident	Energetic	Gifted	Intelligent	Progressive	Trusting
Courageous	Engaging	Good natured	Inviting	Radiant	Youthful

Top 3 personality traits: ....

Brand Values

What values best represent your brand? Choose **TEN** words and narrow them to **THREE**.

Accessibility	*Collaboration*	*Diversity*	*Freedom*	*Integrity*	*Pragmatism*
Accomplishment	*Comfort*	*Duty*	*Friendship*	*Justice*	*Precision*
Aesthetics	*Community*	*Education*	*Harmony*	*Knowledge*	*Privacy*
Affordability	*Compassion*	*Elitism*	*Health*	*Learning*	*Passionate*
Authenticity	*Competition*	*Empowerment*	*Honest*	*Oneness*	*Trust*
Beauty	*Connection*	*Excess*	*Humble*	*Open communication*	*Truth*
Camaraderie	*Creativity*	*Fairness*	*Individuality*	*Over-delivery*	*Wealth*
Cleanliness	*Design*	*Family*	*Innovation*	*Performance*	*Work*

Top 3 brand values:

....

....

....

Brand Imagery

It's time to have some fun. Create a collage using imagery that expresses your brand. This is more on a gut level. Your designer will later take this imagery and evolve it into your marketing tools. Go through magazines and choose photos, font styles, shapes, textures and colors that speak to you when you think of your brand. Keep in mind your primary audience and the feeling word you chose, the three personality traits and three value words that you chose in the last exercise.

What you will need:

1. A piece of white Bristol board
2. A variety of magazines
3. A glue stick

The feeling I want my client or customer to walk away with (page 135): ....

3 top personality traits (page 137): ....

3 top values (page 138): ....

Testing your brand alignment

Why this is important

Use the chart on the next page to test your brand alignment. Now that you have your difference statement, it's important to do an inventory of your current marketing tools to see how well they represent this new direction. (Remember your new statement guides your business now.) You will likely need to take a fresh look at your materials.

With your primary audience in mind, look at each of your current marketing tools and rate how well they align to your new difference statement (1 = not aligned and 10 = bang on). Skip this step, if you are developing a new brand and don't have anything yet. If you need help, ask a graphic designer. You can contact your local art college and enlist the help of a student.

Testing your brand alignment

Instructions: review each of your current marketing tools and rate how well it aligns to your difference statement on pages 127 and 128. (1= very far off and 10 = it works very well)

MY CURRENT MARKETING TOOL	ON A SCALE OF 1-10, HOW WELL DOES THIS ITEM REPRESENT MY NEW DIFFERENCE STATEMENT BY THE WAY IT'S WRITTEN?	ON A SCALE OF 1-10, HOW WELL DOES THIS ITEM REPRESENT MY NEW DIFFERENCE STATEMENT FOR THE WAY IT LOOKS?	ON A SCALE OF 1-10, HOW WELL DOES THIS ITEM REFLECT MY BRAND PERSONALITY WORDS?	ON A SCALE OF 1-10, HOW WELL DOES THIS ITEM REFLECT MY BRAND VALUE WORDS?	ON A SCALE OF 1-10, HOW WELL DOES THIS ITEM COMMUNICATE TO MY PRIMARY AUDIENCE?	TOTAL YOUR SCORE FOR EACH ITEM (OUT OF 50)
Company name						
Logo						
Business card						
Website						
Twitter profile						
Facebook Fan page						
LinkedIn profile						
My photo						
Electronic newsletter						

(ANY ITEM THAT HAS A SCORE OF 30 OR LESS SHOULD BE RECONSIDERED!)

Brand Summary

CONGRATULATIONS! You've done the hard work and now it's time to summarize your learning. This summary is your guiding light and will assist you going forward. You will use it to brief your creative team. When they review your summary, they will know the direction to bring your brand to life. Your brand summary will also help you:

- Speak about your business in a new way.

- Guide the written content for your website and marketing tools.

- Make decisions about all aspects of your business going forward, from hiring people to choosing an office space.

Note: Suppliers are not to use the copy directly from your summary, but use it as a guideline to determine what you're going for and who you're talking to. Hire a good copywriter to help you write content and put it all together. It doesn't have to be expensive and it is important to get the words right (often you can barter).

Your brand summary begins on the next page. To help you fill it out, refer to pages: 27 for your vision, 42 for competition, 127 for your difference statement, 135 for the feeling I want my client or customer to walk away with, 137 brand personality and 138 brand values.

 To create an electronic version of your brand summary that you can email to your suppliers go to: www.knowyourdifference.com/freebonus

www.knowyourdifference.com/freebonus

know your di**ff**erence™   a branding workbook

Brand summary

This brand summary is to be used to inform partners, such as writers, graphic designers and web developers of your company's direction. It is a briefing document and not to be used in any marketing capacity.

You can fill in the following pages by hand and photocopy them or use an electronic version at *www.knowyourdifference.com/freebonus*

Company Name: ....   Date: ....

Tagline: ....

Vision: ....

....

....

....

....

About your *photo*

Make sure to have a professional photo of yourself. Wear clothing and colors that align with your difference. Have your hair and makeup (even men!) professionally done. A great photo makes all the difference. In today's social media world, people want to see who you are so they can relate to you better. A poor photo may give a poor message. I suggest giving your photographer your brand summary to review.

Top 3 competitors (List name, URL and any key observations):

1 ....

2 ....

3 ....

Target audience: ....

1. Primary audience description: ....

....

....

....

2. Secondary audience list: ....

....

....

....

Difference Statement: ....

....

....

....

Credibility Points: ....

1 ....

2 ....

3 ....

The feeling I want my client or customer to walk away with is ....

Three Brand Personality Traits:

1 ....

2 ....

3 ....

Three Brand Values:

1 ....

2 ....

3 ....

Brand imagery:

Make sure to show your brand imagery to your creative team when you meet with them.

Below, record the colors and relevant images from your brand imagery exercise.

....

....

....

....

Target date to launch my new brand: ....

Marketing toolbox to do list (check boxes):

☐ New company or product name(s)

☐ Tagline

☐ Logo

☐ Business cards

☐ Website design

☐ Blog design

☐ Written content for my website

☐ PowerPoint template

☐ Electronic newsletter template

☐ Brochure(s) (print or electronic)

☐ Business portrait

Services I need:

☐ Copywriting

☐ Graphic Design

☐ Website Design

☐ Marketing Strategy

☐ Search Engine Optimization (SEO)

☐ Social Media Strategy

INSIDE DESIGN

Getting your marketing toolbox right
(This segment was co-written with Don Cleland of Cleland Creative)

Why this is important

Now that you know your difference, and have identified what you need in your marketing toolbox, the next step is design. Design will play an important role in how your brand comes to life. Design helps you to further differentiate your business. Design translates your difference statement into something tangible.

People come to me all the time and ask me to look at their website and tell them if it's good. I ask them, *What's your strategy? Who's your audience? Who's your competition? What's your differentiated message?* Often the answer is *"I've never thought of any of that."* It's difficult to assess design without looking at the other criteria, which you've now done. This section will help you to understand how to choose the right designer for your project, how to work effectively with that designer, while staying aligned to your difference statement and how to assess the design that's presented to you. My hope is that this will empower you for the future of your business, as every business needs to rely on creative people throughout its lifespan.

A note about *web designers*

I strongly recommend hiring your graphic designer before a web designer. Most graphic designers today are aligned with a web person. Web designers are not trained in the same way as graphic designers. In my experience, you will get a better end result working with a graphic designer first.

Choosing the right graphic designer

Choosing a good graphic designer is extremely important in the development of your brand. There are dozens of graphic designers around and everyone you know will recommend someone. When desk top publishing became popular, suddenly everyone was selling themselves as a graphic designer. Make sure to work with a designer who has had formal graphic design training at a reputable institution. Spending some time to choose the right person will really pay off in the end.

Look for a designer who has done work in your area of focus. If you are marketing a food product, make sure to choose a designer who has packaging, and in particular, food packaging experience. Packaging food is quite different from packaging electronic equipment! Most designers will gladly send you their portfolio for your review. I recommend starting with three designers and narrowing it down to one. Make sure to have a conversation with each designer to see if you feel aligned to work with them from a personal chemistry standpoint.

How to find a graphic designer

Start with your network and ask friends who have done a great job on their brand. Look for design that you like and find out who did it. That's how I found my designer Megan Hunt. Every major city has a graphic design association you can call for recommendations.

AIGA (www.aiga.org) was founded in 1914 and is the oldest and largest professional membership organization in the United States for graphic design. It has a chapter in every state. In Canada, you can contact the GDC, Society of Graphic Designers of Canada (www.gdc.net) for recommendations. If you are tight on budget, go to a local art college and find out who their top graphic design students are.

Pricing design work

Before you speak to a designer for the first time, send them your brand summary. Make sure you are very clear on what you need, your timing and your budget. If you don't feel comfortable telling them your budget, make sure you have a number in your mind of what you are prepared to spend on design. Don't waste their time, asking for a proposal before you know if they are in your ballpark. Ask for a verbal price range to make sure they're in your ballpark. Once you know you are somewhat aligned with pricing, you can ask them to spell out the scope of the project, the deliverables, schedule and budget. I strongly advise that you do not make your decision based on price alone!

On the following page is a chart to help you make a decision on which designer to use.

The process of working with a designer

We talked a lot about the difference between branding and marketing earlier in the workbook. Design is a separate discipline and good design operates within the context of branding and marketing.

Experienced designers follow a process in order to effectively translate a brand summary into design. Typical development stages in the design process may include research (competitive), concept development (the big idea), design (working out the details) and implementation (applying the brand to tangible media like a business card for example). Your designer should provide you with a detailed *scope of work* and the process they go through before you begin the project.

Note: If you've done a brand imagery board as I recommended earlier in the workbook, show it to your designer and have a discussion on why you chose the imagery, colors and fonts. This will help them get an idea of what resonates well with you. Some designers will show you 20 ideas, but a good designer will show you three strong directions. You may feel like you are getting more for your money by seeing 20. But trust me, you'll be putting yourself in a state of being overwhelmed, confused and making a decision will become very difficult. (Most designers will have worked through dozens of ideas before arriving at the few they show you.)

Remember that the price to design something and the cost to produce it are two separate budgets!

Evaluate three designers using the following chart. Answer yes or no in the boxes.
The one with the most **YES'S** wins.

SELECTION CRITERIA	DESIGNER A	DESIGNER B	DESIGNER C
Are they available to deliver your project within your timeframe?			
Are they in the ballpark of your budget? (verbal estimate)			
Do you have chemistry and can you talk to them easily?			
Do they have an inclusive process that is open to feedback?			
Do they have experience with the product or service you offer?			
Did they graduate from a graphic design program at a reputable institution?			
When you look at their portfolio, have they used type in a pleasing way?			
When you look at their portfolio, have they used color in a pleasing way?			
When you look at their portfolio, is their work clean looking and easy to read?			
When you look at the projects they've worked on, do you get a good feel for the brand?			

Feeling discomfort when you look at design is not always a bad thing. Sometimes you need to step outside your comfort zone in order to create something that will really stand out.

Evaluating the design work presented to you

Design is a highly subjective topic, because it stimulates our senses on an emotional level that at times defies all logic. Good design speaks to us in a way that can move us to action by connecting with our emotions. In this way, the design is said to be *effective.* Good design is anything but a style exercise, which relies on aesthetics alone. Aesthetics are certainly a part of good design, but only when relevant to the message or tone of the brand. Here are some criteria that you can use to evaluate good design:

- *Is it clean looking?*
- *Is the type easy to read?*
- *Does the most important information stand out?*
- *Do the colors feel right for your brand's personality?*
- *How do you feel when you look at it? (Remember your feeling word from your brand summary.)*
- *Does it represent the core values of your business?*
- *If you put it beside your competitors', does it look the same or does it stand out?*

You may want to look at it in a store, if it's a product. Test it out on some friends or form your own informal focus group for feedback. In the end, trust your gut. If you are working with a good designer, all options will be good ones!

Giving your designer feedback

Identifying good design, finding a designer who demonstrates mastery, and understanding how designers work, are all critical aspects in managing the process of applying effective design to your brand. However, without the ability to properly direct the process through constructive feedback, the outcomes of the exercise may be left to chance. Giving feedback throughout the design process, and at the right times, is key to keeping the creative flow on point while ensuring the brand's successful development.

Every designer works a bit differently so make sure to find out from your designer the key points in your project when feedback will be needed.

Moving beyond the love it or hate it paradigm

Many people have a fear of feedback—giving or receiving it. From my perspective, feedback is gold! It allows you to create a much better product. I used to be afraid of it too, but now I love it. The more feedback the better!

Take an active role in your design project. Don't give direction then sit back and wait for your designer to deliver something great. The design process must be collaborative in order to work well. It's a back and forth flow of working together that produces a great result. Make sure to let your designer know what your thought process is. For example, are you the type that doesn't comment right away and needs to sleep on it first? Or do you prefer to react and make decisions immediately? However your thought process, saying you *love it* or *hate it* is not useful to your designer.

Here is the appropriate way to convey your concerns:
- Provide reasons why you feel the way you do. For example, tell your designer your gut reaction.
- Tell your designer what excites you most about the design or what makes you uncomfortable.
- Ask your designer to explain how his or her design concept relates to your brand summary.

Hopefully by now you have a greater appreciation of what goes into the design process. Start to see design in a different way. Try to understand the meaning in certain pieces. When you are buying your groceries, start noticing what stands out about the packaging of a product and ask yourself, why does it stand out to you? If you embrace these techniques, you will notice your confidence increasing when it comes to working with your creative team!

INSIDE WRITING

Why this is important

Just as great design is vital to differentiating your brand, so is writing. In fact, writing and design are interconnected: well written copy supports great design and vice versa. Having your difference clearly articulated makes it memorable.

I highly recommend seeking a professional copywriter's help. Your budget may not be able to afford a professional writer who can write your content from scratch. However, having a professional review and edit your content is advised and worth the investment. Here are a few reasons why:

1. *An experienced copywriter will help you select the right choice of words that best illustrates your difference. So often, entrepreneurs who write their own copy are disappointed when the message they wanted to convey doesn't receive the response they hoped for.*

2. *A professional writer will also help you "trim the fat"—in essence, get rid of superfluous words that only add unnecessary weight to your content. Heavy-weighted content will only confuse your target audience. Clear and concise phrases are memorable. They should call people to action.*

3. *On the opposite side of weighty content is information that is too lean. A copywriter will help you see where there are gaps or holes in the content. Again, a well-articulated difference will attract your target audience.*

About *key words*

Writing for the web is a different ball of wax. Key words are very important to make sure your site is found. When you're creating content for your website, make sure your writer is an experienced website writer and knows how to properly incorporate key words.

As I've noted before, if budget is an issue for you, hire an eager Journalism or English major student from your local university or community college to help you.

When hiring a professional writer, apply the same strategy I outlined for a graphic designer. However, keep the following points in mind.

- There are many different styles of writing: academic, business, narrative or journalistic, just to name a few. When writing short, simple yet compelling content, hiring a copywriter is your best bet. A copywriter's mandate is to help you promote, persuade, inform and influence your target audience, without distorting or twisting the information. Always remember to ask the question *"Is this information aligned with my difference?"*

- A great copywriter should help you *sell* your product or service. They not only write well, but have a good understanding of marketing.

As I mentioned before, a professional chooses the appropriate words or phrases that best reflects your brand and customer. It's also a good idea to choose a writer who is familiar with your industry.

- This point may seem too simple to mention, but it is an important one that many people don't consider: Hire a writer who loves the writing process and is enthusiastic about the craft. Your assignment is not "just another job" to the writer, but an opportunity for him or her to help you and your business succeed. Your writer must have your utmost interests at heart.

- And finally, when you read the content written for you, ask yourself if it excites you. Does it fill you with pride and a sense of achievement when you see *your difference* in writing? I encourage you to show the written content to others to get their feedback, whether they are from your target audience or simply people you trust.

Naming Your Brand

Ready to make a name for yourself? It's more than a fun creative exercise. Naming is an important part of your business strategy. The right name can get you noticed. The wrong name can doom you to obscurity.

Fundamentally, your name should convey two things: your **DIFFERENCE** and your **PERSONALITY**.

There are many approaches to naming, but all fall into two basic categories: names that have an inherent meaning and names that take on meaning over time. There are pros and cons to each.

When a name already means something to your audience...

- You can communicate your difference very quickly. A descriptive name can influence the decision to buy in the absence of any other marketing. Calling yourself Reliable Taxi might just get you more calls.
- You may spend less time and marketing dollars to build awareness of what you're all about.
- Your name may be easier to remember and easier to spell than a coined name.
- You can combine familiar words to make your name more distinct (FlexGuard, Pathstone)
- An expressive name, such as Acrobat, gives you the advantage of positive associations without being overly limiting in meaning.

But...

- A simple descriptive name is more difficult to distinguish in a crowded marketplace. Was it Reliable Taxi, or Dependable Taxi? They may end up calling your competitor.
- A descriptive name may be limited to a single positive association. If you are Zen Yoga, will you be alienating people who take yoga for fitness?
- Planning to expand to new markets? What does the name mean in French or Spanish? Maybe nothing. Maybe worse.
- Planning to launch products, services or operating divisions under your brand name? A longer descriptive name may be cumbersome to deal with.

- Over time, your name may not align with the offering as your business evolves. You may be Breakfast Nook today but decide in future to serve the dinner crowd. Oops, you're stuck.
- Expressive names are more distinct, but may have different associations for different people. Is Acrobat a good name? If it makes you think of flexibility and skill, yes. If it makes you think about swinging around without a net, no.
- "Dictionary" words are often not distinct and rarely available. Even blended words, such as GlobalNet and EnVista are increasingly difficult to trademark. Everyone wants to be Apple. But remember that Apple got into the game thirty years ago.
- Your name may not be available as a desirable domain name.

When a name may not mean anything to your audience...

- In a world where competition is fierce, it often pays to be different.

- An original name can be a great ice breaker. When people ask, "What does your name mean?" You have an opportunity to tell your story. Foreign and Latin words are a good direction to explore, as they have an inherent meaning, but not one that is widely understood.

- If your name has no inherent meaning, you have greater control over what it means to others.

- You increase the chances that your name will stay with you as you grow and diversify.

- With a distinct name, you can launch new offerings under your master brand using only a generic descriptor. Artanis becomes Artanis Express or Artanis Hosting.

- A distinct name is easier to trademark.

- Your name may be effective in multiple languages.

- A desirable domain name (www.name.com) is more likely to be available. For many businesses that operate on the Internet, the business name is synonymous with the domain name.

But...

- You may need to invest more time and marketing dollars to build the desired associations with your brand. Consider adding a tagline that underscores the meaning of the name *(e.g., Qualif—Working to improve quality of life in your community).*

- If your name is open to interpretation, it may be open to misinterpretation.

- If your name is difficult to remember or difficult to pronounce, it can cause frustration and confusion.

- If your name relies on an unusual spelling, you may be more difficult to find in industry listings and search engines.

While your business name should capture your difference, you shouldn't expect it to communicate everything you want to say about your brand. It is only one of the tools in your marketing toolbox. Your name, tagline, logo and visual style will work together to create an overall impression about your brand. Simple is better.

About your *URL*

Your URL is your web address. Make sure your web address is easy to spell and remember. If the exact name of your company isn't available, try to come up with another name that still makes it memorable and easy to spell. (Think of the frustration when typing web addresses that are full of hyphens and other punctuation.)

Giving direction to create names

Whether you're developing a business name yourself or briefing a professional who will do it for you, (many writers do naming) you should have a creative brief. It details the criteria that will guide name generation and will help you to gauge the appropriateness of the proposed names. The creative brief refers back to your brand summary, answering the following:

- What is your difference?
- Who are your primary and secondary audiences?
- What are the brand experiences (what you want the audience to feel)?
- What are your brand personality traits and brand values?
- Are there any sensitivities (words, perceptions, etc.) that you need to avoid?
- Are there any types of names you don't like or just won't work for your business?
- What names have you come across that you really like? (They can be direct competitors or in a different industry.)

- Does the name need to work in more than one language?
- Will the name need to accommodate sub-brands (products, services or operating divisions)?
- Does the name need to be available outright as a .com? Or can you play with the full name to get a domain that's available?

If you are renaming a business:

- Is there equity in the current name? Is there value in retaining elements of that name?
- What change in the business should the new name convey, either in meaning or tone (e.g., from product-based to consultant-based)?
- Does the name have to work with an existing logo or tagline?

When you have the answers to these questions, use them to create a checklist for assessing the names you want to consider.

Add these other functional attributes to the checklist:

☐ Is distinct within its competitive set
☐ Projects clearly and uniquely
☐ Is memorable and easily recalled
☐ Is legally ownable within its competitive environment

Kinds of names

A DESCRIPTIVE NAME conveys one or more *rational attributes* of the brand: Safeguard Systems, Rapid Mobile Energy, Reliance Insurance.

AN EXPRESSIVE NAME conveys characteristics of the brand through association, conveying the emotional attributes of the brand: Anthem, Tango, Amazon, Bridgewater, Energy Star.

A COINED NAME is an invented name that may or may not have an inherent meaning. Examples: Imeris, Finto, Antrizan

know your di*fference*™ **a branding workbook**

Name evaluation scorecard

On a scale of 1-10 rank the names individually (1 being weak and 10 being strong), then total your scores.

Suggestion: ask clients or friends to help with the ranking.

	NAMING CRITERIA	OPTION 1	OPTION 2	OPTION 3	OPTION 4
1	Is your first impression of the name strong?				
2	Does it sound/look good?				
3	Is it easy to read/pronounce?				
4	Use it in different sentences. Does it feel right?				
5	Is it distinct within its competitive set?				
6	Does it relate to your difference statement?				
7	Does it relate to the primary benefits of the company/product/service?				
8	Does it speak to the primary audience?				
9	Is it memorable?				
10	Is it available? (domain and registration)				
	TOTAL SCORE				

GET THE WORD OUT!

Why this is important

Why is getting the word out important? It speaks for itself. By now you **know your difference**™ and you have good marketing tools to communicate your difference. After all this hard work, it's time to tell everyone! The most important thing to remember is your primary audience. The more targeted you are in getting the word out, the more your message will be heard.

You've got your marketing tools ready. It's important to go about getting the word out in a thoughtful, methodical way. Be consistent—slow and steady wins the race.

There are a number of ways to get the word out about your business. I will highlight the most effective ones to get you started.

Inspiration Box

"Successful people take action." —*JACK CANFIELD*

1. **NETWORKING EVENTS.** Face-to-face interaction is still a very powerful way to connect with your target audience and leave a lasting impression. Make sure to go to events or join associations where you will find your target audience. Remember to bring your business cards and be comfortable with talking about your business and your difference.

2. **ONLINE MARKETING.** Learn as much as you can about the benefits of online marketing and how, if done well, can drive traffic to your website. For example, your site should have a place where visitors can "opt-in" or fill in their email address to get information for free, such as a special report, or subscribe to your newsletter. Your opt-in is very important as this will build your mailing list and so you have a large group to market to. You want to have people visiting your site because they find your information valuable. Consider having your website optimized. A good search engine optimization strategist will work with you to ensure that you are ranked high on the different search engines like Google.

3. **SOCIAL MEDIA.** Twitter, Facebook, LinkedIn or your own blog are all powerful ways to get the word out about your business. These avenues are called social media for a reason: they allow you to connect and share information while endorsing your business. The most important point to remember is whatever you share, make it relevant, timely and consistent. You want to be perceived as an "expert" in your field and convey that what you have to say is worth knowing. It is also important to have your social media presence linked to your website.

4. **YOUTUBE.** Whether it is a VideoBio, showcasing your product or service to the world, or another video concept, YouTube will help you spread the word. It is considered to be the most powerful public relations and advertising tool for the individual. If you decide to use this channel of communications, it's important to make sure the video is of good quality and that your information is tight, concise, and visually appealing.

When getting the word out, remember to stay aligned with your brand summary, and once again, take your time. You don't have to implement everything at once. Investigate what will work best for you and your business. Consider hiring a marketing specialist to help you. Again, like designers, there are lots of marketing specialists out there. Do your research and make sure to choose one with a good track record and experience in marketing for entrepreneurs and small businesses. Ask for references!

Deliver on your promise!

One more thing that needs to be mentioned. Make sure you can deliver on what you are promising. Think of all those brands you know of that offer great things but don't deliver. Before you start to get the word out, get your ducks in a row. Whether you're marketing a product or service, make sure that you deliver a great experience!

Action plan

Make a list of your next action steps and schedule the dates for completion using the chart on the following page.

A word of caution about advertising: Advertising can be very expensive. If you choose to advertise, make sure you have a well thought-out strategy and that you are prepared financially to commit to repeating your ad on an ongoing basis. Always keep your primary and secondary audiences in mind. Advertisers always have specifications (or specs) on who their audience is. Ask for their specs and see if your audience is part of their group. As an alternative to advertising, I'm an advocate of using a PR campaign to get your business into the media.

ACTION STEP	COMPLETION DATE

know your *difference*™ a branding workbook

Story: **Redefining my brand**

NATHALIE MCFARLANE
BUSINESS LAWYER, Positive Impact Law
www.positiveimpactlaw.com

I left the corporate world to open a private law practice. I knew I wanted to serve socially conscious enterprises and that my service offer was unique, but when it came to identifying and expressing it, I found it challenging to do. I understood the concept of branding; however, my issue was "How do I go about applying it to my own law firm."

Rhonda retained me to trademark **know your difference**™ and copyright the workbook at the same time I was grappling with clearly defining my target market and branding the business. I went to her website and saw the way she described her services through her business name and how it really captured what I needed to do and what I was trying to accomplish.

I decided to take Rhonda's workshop and it was the start of really identifying and creating a vision and brand for my business. Going through the workbook got my mind churning. I was also able to get ideas through interacting with other participants in the workshop—ideas that would speak directly to my difference. Her process ignited a flow of considerations I hadn't thought of before or probably wouldn't have thought of independently. It helped me to transform what initially was a vague business idea and made it into something clear, that I could confidently articulate and approach the target market I wanted to serve with. She helped me narrow it down and express it in a way that was marketable.

When it came to designing my marketing tools, Rhonda introduced me to a graphic designer. Both Rhonda and the designer felt that the name I had for my firm wasn't differentiated enough. There were other law firms calling themselves by similar names. This inspired me to create a new name that truly speaks to my service offer and is a better reflection of who I am. That was another important piece of the puzzle that fell into place through the process I went through with **know your difference**™.

Currently, I'm focusing on the business model and the back-end ideas of how I intend to operate. But in terms of marketing, it's just a matter of finding the locations where my target market is and letting them know that I'm out there for them.

Story: **Standing out from the rest**

ANNABELLE FELL
REGISTERED SOCIAL WORKER & FOUNDER OF
Launch Kids, I Call the Shots, and *In Motion*

As a social worker and entrepreneur with a new idea, I knew my offer was unique but had to figure out how to package it in a way that would stand out from all the other social workers, psychologists and coaches who work with kids and families. Rhonda and I worked together to make that happen.

I had been working on my new business for six months before I met Rhonda and had a lot of ideas but didn't know where to focus the message. She helped me determine where to start, how to build on that foundation, how to further develop my ideas and come up with new ones.

Rhonda distilled the key points of what I had to say and helped me simplify some of the messages I was putting out there to people. We got rid of a lot of the noise and kept what was most essential.

My business fills a gap in the market for kids, teens and young adults who are really trying to understand who they are. My offer concentrates on prevention instead of treatment. There are very few practitioners in the field right now focusing on this area. I knew I was different but wasn't sure what to tell my clients. After going through Rhonda's Insight Interview process, I was able to articulate my skill set and background more explicitly, based on what my clients perceived to be my strengths. We came up with the three things that make me most credible from their point of view.

Rhonda also assisted me in creating a statement that I could put on my business cards, which explains exactly what I do. We determined that there would be three programs for three different age groups and each program would have its own name: **LAUNCH KIDS**, for kids under 12; **I CALL THE SHOTS**, for teens; and **IN MOTION** for young adults. Rhonda gave me enough information that I could brief my graphic designer and come up with a new identity. She got me into shape. She understood what I was trying to accomplish.

I left a job to start my own business. I am dedicated to empowering kids, teens and young adults with the self-knowledge and skills they need to manage life's challenges and reach their greatest potential.

I am pleased to say that business is booming!

know your di*ff*erence™ a branding workbook

CONGRATULATIONS!

You now have new strategies for growing your business with a powerful brand. Are you now asking one of these common questions?

How can I…

- Get Rhonda's direct input on my business and my brand?
- Get group support to work through these steps and have my questions answered?
- Create a cost effective website that I can update myself?
- Find the perfect graphic designer and website developer to help me along the way?
- Come up with unique marketing ideas that actually work?
- Use everything I've done here to feed into my business development process?

There are **THREE** opportunities to accelerate your progress:

1. YOUR BRAND BREAKTHROUGH: Accelerate your success with individual support from Rhonda in a small group coaching setting. You'll benefit from direct input from Rhonda and her unique insights to your brand. This program ensures quick advancement, steady progress and ongoing support from Rhonda and a group of like minded brand builders.

2. YOUR BRAND BOOST: The only branding course on-line! Improve your understanding of the book by going deeper into each chapter with special insights, stories and insider information. For advanced learning and access to great resources, discounts on graphic design and web development and access to the world's first branding mastermind group!

3. YOUR BRAND BRIEFING: Listen to important facts about the 6 steps to Brand Clarity to enhance your journey through the book! Gain access to the branding mastermind group.

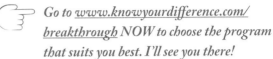

Go to www.knowyourdifference.com/breakthrough NOW to choose the program that suits you best. I'll see you there!

www.knowyourdifference.com/breakthrough

RECOMMENDED READING AND RESOURCES

Crush It!

By Gary Vaynerchuck

A great explanation on how to use social
media, such as Facebook and Twitter, to build your brand.

The Success Principles

By Jack Canfield

How to get from where you are to where you want to be.

ZAG, The #1 Strategy of High-Performance Brands

By Marty Neumeier

A quick and easy read about creating a brand.

Secrets of the Millionaire Mind

By T. Harv Eker

Mastering the inner game of wealth.

Instant Income

By Janet Switzer

Full of great marketing advice and ideas.

The Artist's Way

By Julia Cameron

If you're feeling stuck or blocked creatively.

The Hoffman Institute

If you're feeling stuck in general.

www.hoffmaninstitute.org

A Year of Possibilities

By Helen Valleau

A visioning workbook to move you into action
and create a life of purpose and passion.

www.ayearofpossibilities.com